IN THE WORDS OF NEIL DEGRASSE TYSON

THE INSPIRING VOICE OF SCIENCE

FRANK JOHNSON

Copyright © 2014 Frank Johnson

All rights reserved.

ISBN: 1505440599
ISBN-13: 978-1505440591

DISCLAIMER

Although every effort has been taken to ensure the accuracy of all quotes in this book, the author apologises in the event of any mistakes.

CONTENTS

Introduction	1
Himself	3
Science	13
Innovation	27
Kids	33
Astronomy & the Universe	37
General Thoughts & Opinions	51
Mankind	57
Philosophy	63
Politics	69
Religion	73

INTRODUCTION

One of the most inspirational voices in science today, Neil deGrasse Tyson is somebody with a contagious passion for his field of work. Although not as well known outside America (speaking from the point of view of an Englishman myself), he is one of the few members of the scientific community who is truly able to effectively communicate complex concepts to the common man.

Tyson's likeable character and obvious enthusiasm for all things space-related have undoubtedly contributed largely to his success not just as an astrophysicist but also a public figure.

Although fondly claimed by the atheist community, Tyson (as you will see) does not consider himself to be an atheist. In fact, he doesn't like labels at all, although it is clear from his own words that agnosticism would be closest to the mark.

FRANK JOHNSON

Tyson has a lot to say on a variety of topics. What really comes across when listening to him speak is his total honesty and complete integrity.

This book brings together some of his most interesting comments on a number of different subjects.

HIMSELF

"As an educator, I try to get people to be fundamentally curious and to question ideas that they might have or that are shared by others. In that state of mind, they have earned a kind of inoculation against the fuzzy thinking of these weird ideas floating around out there."

*

"I'm often asked - and occasionally in an accusatory way - 'Are you atheist?' And it's like, 'You know, the only 'ist' I am is a scientist, all right?' I don't associate with movements. I'm not an 'ism.' I just - I think for myself."

*

"I've been a minimalist my whole life, even if you wouldn't know it from my office."

*

"I was transformed by picking up a pair of binoculars and looking up, and that's hard to do for a city kid because when you look up you just see buildings - and really, your first thought is to look in people's windows. So to look out of the space - out of living space - and look up to the sky, binoculars go far, literally and figuratively."

*

"I have a personal philosophy in life: If somebody else can do something that I'm doing, they should do it. And what I want to do is find things that would represent a unique contribution to the world - the contribution that only I, and my portfolio of talents, can make happen. Those are my priorities in life."

*

"I've spent quality time in the aerospace community, with my service on two presidential commissions, but at heart, I'm an academic. Being an academic means I don't wield power over person, place or thing. I don't command armies; I don't lead labor unions. All I have is the power of thought."

*

"Every day, I wake up and I say, 'Why... how... did I end up with 1.7 million Twitter followers?' It's freaky to me, every day, but that tells me that there's an appetite out there that had previously been underserved. There's an inner geek in us all, an inner bit of curiosity that people are discovering, and they like it."

*

"As an American, I grew up in an era where we led the world in everything. Everything!"

*

"While I'm a big fan of science fiction, especially as rendered in expensive Hollywood blockbusters, it's the real universe that calls to me."

*

"I've known from long ago that the universe was calling me. If you were one of those annoying adults that said, 'Oh, what are you gonna be when you grow up?' I would say, 'Astrophysicist.' And then they'd walk away real quickly."

*

"I lose sleep at night wondering whether we are intelligent enough to figure out the universe. I don't know."

*

"All tweets are tasty. Any tweet anybody writes is tasty. So, I try to have each tweet not simply be informative, but have some outlook, some perspective that you might not otherwise had."

*

"My parents didn't know much science; in fact, they didn't know science at all. But they could recognize a science book when they saw it, and they spent a lot of time at bookstores, combing the remainder tables for science books to buy for me. I had one of the biggest libraries of any kid in school, built on books that cost 50 cents or a dollar."

*

"I get enormous satisfaction from knowing I'm doing something for society."

*

"Although I'm not actually embarrassed by this, I tend not to read books that have awesome movies made from them, regardless of how well or badly the movie represented the actual written story."

*

"I always try to get people a different outlook. When you do that, people take ownership of the information. They don't ever have to reference me because, I'd like to believe as an educator, I'm empowering them to have those thoughts themselves."

*

FRANK JOHNSON

"I was born the same week NASA was founded, so we're the same age and feel some of the same pains, joys, and frustrations."

*

"If you only think of me during Black History Month, I must be failing as an educator and as an astrophysicist."

*

"I was an aspiring astrophysicist, and that's how I defined myself, not by my skin color. People didn't treat me as someone with science ambitions. They treated me as someone they thought was going to mug them, or who was a shoplifter."

*

"Half of my library are old books because I like seeing how people thought about their world at their time. So that I don't get bigheaded about something we just discovered and I can be humble about where we might go next. Because you can see who got stuff right and most of the people who got stuff wrong."

*

"I don't want people to say, 'Something is true because Tyson says it is true.' That's not critical thinking."

*

"For me at age 11, I had a pair of binoculars and looked up to the moon, and the moon wasn't just bigger, it was better. There were mountains and valleys and craters and shadows. And it came alive."

*

"I study the universe. It's the second oldest profession. People have been looking up for a long time."

*

"There is always a place I can take someone's curiosity and land where they end up enlightened when we're done. That's my challenge as an educator. No one is dumb who is curious. The people who don't ask questions remain clueless throughout their lives."

*

"You've never seen me debate anybody. On anything. Ever. My investment of time, as an educator, in my judgment, is best served teaching people how to think about the world around them. Teach them how to pose a question. How to judge whether one thing is true versus another. What the laws of physics say."

*

"I never got into 'Star Wars.' Maybe because they made no attempt to portray real physics. At all."

*

"For me, the most fascinating interface is Twitter. I have odd cosmic thoughts every day and I realized I could hold them to myself or share them with people who might be interested."

*

"I don't comment on the physics errors of 'Star Wars,' all right. I just - you let that one go."

*

"I'm not as famous as Stephen Hawking, but certainly in the U.S., I have a very high profile for a scientist. It is an awesome responsibility, one that I don't shoulder lightly."

SCIENCE

"I like to believe that science is becoming mainstream. It should have never been something that sort of geeky people do and no one else thinks about. Whether or not, it will always be what geeky people do. It should, as a minimum, be what everybody thinks about because science is all around us."

*

"We think scientific literacy flows out of how many science facts can you recite rather than how was your brain wired for thinking. And it's the brain wiring that I'm more interested in rather than the facts that come out of the curriculum or the lesson plan that's been proposed."

*

"Science literacy is the artery through which the solutions of tomorrow's problems flow."

*

"If you're a scientist, and you have to have an answer, even in the absence of data, you're not going to be a good scientist."

*

"The methods and tools of science perennially breach barriers, granting me confidence that our epic march of insight into the operations of nature will continue without end."

*

"We explore our environment, more than we are compelled to utter poetry, when we're toddlers. We start doing that later. Before that happens, every child is a scientist."

*

"Any time scientists disagree, it's because we have insufficient data. Then we can agree on what kind of data to get; we get the data; and the data solves the problem. Either I'm right, or you're right, or we're both wrong. And we move on. That kind of conflict resolution does not exist in politics or religion."

*

"You will never find scientists leading armies into battle. You just won't. Especially not astrophysicists - we see the biggest picture there is. We understand how small we are in the cosmos. We understand how fragile and temporary our existence is here on Earth."

*

"Scientists in different disciplines don't speak the same language. They publish in different journals. It's like the United Nations: You come together, but no one speaks the same language, so you need some translators."

*

"It was unthinkable not long ago that a biologist or

paleontologist would be at the same conference as an astrophysicist. Now we have accumulated so much data in each of these branches of science as it relates to origins that we have learned that no one discipline can answer questions of origins alone."

*

"Carl Sagan spoke fluently between biology and geology and astrophysics and physics. If you move fluently across those boundaries, you realize that science is everywhere; science is not something you can step around or sweep under the rug."

*

"What are we promoting in society? Well-behaved automatons that spew back what they learned in a book. That's not science. You can get a parrot to do that."

*

"Innovations in science and technology are the engines of the 21st-century economy; if you care about the wealth and health of your nation tomorrow, then you'd better rethink how you allocate taxes to fund science. The federal budget needs to recognize this."

*

"Most gravity has no known origin. Is it some exotic particle? Nobody knows. Is dark energy responsible for expansion of the universe? Nobody knows."

*

"I try to show the public that chemistry, biology, physics, astrophysics is life. It is not some separate subject that you have to be pulled into a corner to be taught about."

*

"As history has shown, pure science research ultimately ends up applying to something. We just don't know it at the time."

*

"Part of what it is to be scientifically-literate, it's not simply, 'Do you know what DNA is? Or what the Big Bang is?' That's an aspect of science literacy. The biggest part of it is do you know how to think about information that's presented in front of you."

*

"Physics is the only profession in which prophecy is not only accurate but routine."

*

"Keep in mind that if you take a tour through a hospital and look at every machine with on and off switch that is brought into the service of diagnosing the human condition, that machine is based on principles of physics discovered by a physicist in a machine designed by an engineer."

*

"The center line of science literacy - which not many people tell you, but I feel this strongly, and I will go to my grave making this point - is how you think."

*

"When we see animals doing remarkable things, how

do we know if we're simply seeing tricks or signs of real intelligence? Are talented animals just obeying commands, or do they have some kind of deeper understanding? One of the biggest challenges for animal researchers is to come up with tests that can distinguish between the two."

*

"There is no science in this world like physics. Nothing comes close to the precision with which physics enables you to understand the world around you. It's the laws of physics that allow us to say exactly what time the sun is going to rise. What time the eclipse is going to begin. What time the eclipse is going to end."

*

"I claim that all those who think they can cherry-pick science simply don't understand how science works. That's what I claim. And if they did, they'd be less prone to just assert that somehow scientists are clueless."

*

"All the traditional STEM fields, the science,

technology, engineering, and math fields, are stoked when you dream big in an agency such as NASA."

*

"Where there's water on Earth, you find life as we know it. So if you find water somewhere else, it becomes a remarkable draw to look closer to see if life of any kind is there, even if it's bacterial, which would be extraordinary for the field of biology."

*

"As a citizen, as a public scientist, I can tell you that Einstein essentially overturned a so strongly established paradigm of science, whereas Darwin didn't really overturn a science paradigm."

*

"In nature, when you conduct science, it is the natural world that is the ultimate decider in what is true and what is not."

*

"One of the greatest features of science is that it doesn't matter where you were born, and it doesn't matter what the belief systems of your parents might have been: If you perform the same experiment that someone else did, at a different time and place, you'll get the same result."

*

"The caricature of science is that we hold tight to the theories we have, and shun challenges to them. That's just not true. In fact, we hold our highest rewards for those scientists who can prove others wrong. And by the way, they are famous in their own lifetimes. We don't wait until they're dead."

*

"I'm on a crusade to get movie directors to get their science right because, more often than they believe, the science is more extraordinary than anything they can invent."

*

"I want to know what dark matter and dark energy are comprised of. They remain a mystery, a complete mystery. No one is any closer to solving the problem than when these two things were discovered."

*

"I can't tell you how many people say they were turned off from science because of a science teacher that completely sucked out all the inspiration and enthusiasm they had for the course."

*

"Science is basically an inoculation against charlatans."

*

"In science, if you don't do it, somebody else will. Whereas in art, if Beethoven didn't compose the 'Ninth Symphony,' no one else before or after is going to compose the 'Ninth Symphony' that he composed; no one else is going to paint 'Starry Night' by van Gogh."

*

"The very nature of science is discoveries, and the best of those discoveries are the ones you don't expect."

*

"The theory of evolution, like the theory of gravity, is a scientific fact."

*

"Science is an enterprise that should be cherished as an activity of the free human mind. Because it transforms who we are, how we live, and it gives us an understanding of our place in the universe."

*

"You have people who believe they are scientifically literate but, in fact, are not. And I don't mind if you're not scientifically literate, but just admit that to yourself, so that you'll know, and perhaps you can take a first step to try to eradicate that."

*

"Pretty much every plant and animal alive today is the result of eons of natural cross-breeding."

*

"People who are scientists today are scientists in spite of the system, typically, not because of it."

*

"Let's say intelligence is your ability to compose poetry, symphonies, do art, math and science. Chimps can't do any of that, yet we share 99 percent DNA. Everything that we are, that distinguishes us from chimps, emerges from that one-percent difference."

*

"Darwin's theory of evolution is a framework by which we understand the diversity of life on Earth. But there is no equation sitting there in Darwin's 'Origin of Species' that you apply and say, 'What is this species going to look like in 100 years or 1,000 years?' Biology isn't there yet with that kind of predictive precision."

*

IN THE WORDS OF NEIL DEGRASSE TYSON

"If a scientist is not befuddled by what they're looking at, then they're not a research scientist."

INNOVATION

"For most of human civilization, the pace of innovation has been so slow that a generation might pass before a discovery would influence your life, culture or the conduct of nations."

*

"One of the symptoms of an absence of innovation is the fact that you lose your jobs. Everyone else catches up with you. They can do what you do better than you or cheaper than you. And in a multinational corporate-free market enterprise, it is the company's obligation to take the factory to a place where they can make it more cheaply."

*

"NASA has spin-offs, and it's a huge and very impressive list, including accurate and affordable LASIK eye surgery."

*

"If you're going to lead a space frontier, it has to be government; it'll never be private enterprise. Because the space frontier is dangerous, and it's expensive, and it has unquantified risks. And under those conditions, you cannot establish a capital-market evaluation of that enterprise. You can't get investors."

*

"Computers have proved to be formidable chess players. In fact, they've beaten our top human chess champions."

*

"Once you have an innovation culture, even those who are not scientists or engineers - poets, actors, journalists - they, as communities, embrace the meaning of what it is to be scientifically literate. They embrace the concept of an innovation culture. They vote in ways that promote it. They don't fight science and they don't fight technology."

*

"Whether or not people go into space or serve the space industry, they will have the sensitivity to those fields necessary to stimulate unending innovation in the technological fields, and it's that innovation in the 21st century that will drive tomorrow's economies."

*

"Dreams about the future are always filled with gadgets."

*

"To make any future that we dreamt up real requires creative scientists, engineers, and technologists to make it happen. If people are not within your midst who dream about tomorrow - with the capacity to bring tomorrow into the present - then the country might as well just recede back into the cave because that's where we're headed."

*

"With regard to robots, in the early days of robots people said, 'Oh, let's build a robot' and what's the first thought? You make a robot look like a human and do human things. That's so 1950s. We are so past that."

*

"I see all this talk about jobs going overseas as a symptom of the absence of innovation. And the absence of innovation is a symptom of there being no major national priority to advance a frontier."

*

"When you innovate, you create new industries that then boost your economy. And when you create new industries and that becomes part of your culture, your jobs can't go overseas because no one else has figured out how to do it yet."

*

"The urge to miniaturize electronics did not exist before the space program. I mean our grandparents had radios that was furniture in the living room.

Nobody at the time was saying, 'Gee, I want to carry that in my pocket.' Which is a non-thought."

*

"Ever since the Industrial Revolution, investments in science and technology have proved to be reliable engines of economic growth. If homegrown interest in those fields is not regenerated soon, the comfortable lifestyle to which Americans have become accustomed will draw to a rapid close."

*

"The only way you can invent tomorrow is if you break out of the enclosure that the school system has provided for you by the exams written by people who are trained in another generation."

KIDS

"Kids should be allowed to break stuff more often. That's a consequence of exploration. Exploration is what you do when you don't know what you're doing. That's what scientists do every day."

*

"Adults, who outnumber kids four or five to one, are in charge. We wield the resources, run the world, and completely thwart kids' creativity."

*

"The problem is not scientifically illiterate kids; it is scientifically illiterate adults. Kids are born curious about the natural world. They are always turning over rocks, jumping with two feet into mud puddles and playing with the tablecloth and fine china."

*

"Kids are born curious about the world. What adults primarily do in the presence of kids is unwittingly thwart the curiosity of children."

*

"There's a lot of memorization that goes on in school. You memorize vocabulary words and all these sorts of things."

*

"You can't train kids in a world where adults have no concept of what science literacy is. The adults are gonna squash the creativity that would manifest itself, because they're clueless about what it and why it matters. But science can always benefit from the more brains there are that are thinking about it - but that's true for any field."

*

"I'm often asked by parents what advice can I give them to help get kids interested in science? And I have only one bit of advice. Get out of their way. Kids are born curious. Period."

*

"I don't care what town you're born in, what city, what country. If you're a child, you are curious about your environment. You're overturning rocks. You're plucking leaves off of trees and petals off of flowers, looking inside, and you're doing things that create disorder in the lives of the adults around you."

*

"Let me tell you something about full moons: kids don't care about full moons. They'll play in a full moon, no worries at all. They only get scared of magic or werewolves from stupid adults and their stupid adult stories."

ASTRONOMY & THE UNIVERSE

"Asteroids have us in our sight. The dinosaurs didn't have a space program, so they're not here to talk about this problem. We are, and we have the power to do something about it. I don't want to be the embarrassment of the galaxy, to have had the power to deflect an asteroid, and then not, and end up going extinct."

*

"Let's find a new way to think about the entire taxonomy of solar system objects, and not clutch to this concept of 'planet,' which, of course, only ever meant, 'Do you move against the background stars, regardless of what you're made of?'"

*

"We account for one-sixth of the forces of gravity we see in the universe. There is no known objects accounting for most of the effective gravity in the universe. Something is making stuff move that is not anything we have ever touched."

*

"Space exploration is a force of nature unto itself that no other force in society can rival."

*

"The supermoon is a 16-inch pizza compared with a 15-inch pizza. It's a slightly bigger moon; I ain't using the adjective 'supermoon.'"

*

"If Mars formed life, then life on Earth could have been seeded by life on Mars, making every life form on Earth descended from Martians."

*

"Venus has a runaway greenhouse effect. I kind of want to know what happened there because we're twirling knobs here on Earth without knowing the consequences of it. Mars once had running water. It's bone dry today. Something bad happened there as well."

*

"Those who see the cosmic perspective as a depressing outlook, they really need to reassess how they think about the world. Because when I look up in the universe, I know I'm small but I'm also big. I'm big because I'm connected to the universe, and the universe is connected to me."

*

"Private enterprise can never lead a space frontier. It's not possible because a space frontier is expensive, it has unknown risks and it has unquantified risks."

*

"Some asteroids have us in their sights. Be nice to sort of go near them and find out what they're made of, possibly tag their ears so they're always broadcasting to us their location. In case one of their trajectories head straight for us, we'll know well in advance to do something about it."

*

"The Venus transit is not a spectacle the way a total solar eclipse is a spectacle."

*

"I don't want to be the embarrassment of the galaxy to have had the power to deflect an asteroid, and then not and end up going extinct. We'd be the laughingstock of the aliens of the cosmos if that were the case."

*

"There's something about witnessing something in the sky that makes people think they're seeing something unique or special. I don't really understand the psychology of it, to be honest."

*

"I claim that space is part of our culture. You've heard complaints that nobody knows the names of the astronauts, that nobody gets excited about launches, that nobody cares anymore except people in the industry. I don't believe that for a minute."

*

"The solar system should be viewed as our backyard, not as some sequence of destinations that we do one at a time."

*

"I want people to see that the cosmic perspective is simultaneously honest about the universe we live in and uplifting, when we realize how far we have come and how wonderful is this world of ours."

*

"Any astrophysicist does not feel small looking up at the universe; we feel large."

*

"'Cosmos' wouldn't deserve its place in primetime evening network television were it not a landscape on which compelling stories were told. People, when they watch TV in the evening, want to see stories, and science simply tells the best stories."

*

"Our galaxy, the Milky Way, is one of 50 or 100 billion other galaxies in the universe. And with every step, every window that modern astrophysics has opened to our mind, the person who wants to feel like they're the center of everything ends up shrinking."

*

"There's a lot to do in space. I want to learn more about the greenhouse effect on Venus, about whether there was life on Mars, about the environment in which Earth and the Sun is immersed, the behavior of the Sun."

*

"Space only becomes ordinary when the frontier is no longer being breached."

*

"The chances that your tombstone will read 'Killed by Asteroid' are about the same as they'd be for 'Killed in Airplane Crash.'"

*

"If you slid Pluto to where Earth is right now, heat from the sun would evaporate that ice, and it would grow a tail. Now that's no kind of behavior for a planet."

*

"If you want a nation to have space exploration ambitions, you've got to send humans."

*

"Do you realize that if you fall into a black hole, you will see the entire future of the Universe unfold in front of you in a matter of moments and you will emerge into another space-time created by the singularity of the black hole you just fell into?"

*

"One of the things that fascinates me most is when people are so charmed by the universe that it becomes part of their artistic output."

*

"If the United States commits to the goal of reaching Mars, it will almost certainly do so in reaction to the progress of other nations - as was the case with NASA, the Apollo program, and the project that became the International Space Station."

*

"I'm baffled all the time. We don't know what's driving 96% of the universe. Everybody you know and love and heard of and think about and see in the night sky through a telescope: four percent of the universe."

*

"I'm fascinated by the deaths of stars and the havoc

they wreak on their environments."

*

"All the nine-planet people out there: Get over it. There's eight."

*

"Space enthusiasts are the most susceptible demographic to delusion that I have ever seen."

*

"The partisanship surrounding space exploration and the retrenching of U.S. space policy are part of a more general trend: the decline of science in the United States. As its interest in science wanes, the country loses ground to the rest of the industrialized world in every measure of technological proficiency."

*

"There are a lot of things you can do in space, and space essentially is unlimited resources. We are climbing over ourselves here looking for the next source of energy. The universe has an unlimited source of energy."

*

"If we find life out there, and it's not us, we will deem it not intelligent. But what may be equally as likely is that we find life that's vastly more intelligent than we are. If that's the case, we are putty in their hands."

*

"If you get asteroids about a kilometer in size, those are large enough and carry enough energy into our system to disrupt transportation, communication, the food chains, and that can be a really bad day on Earth."

*

"All Plutophiles are based in America. If you go to other countries, they have much less of an attachment to either the existence or preservation of Pluto as a planet. Once you investigate that, you find out that Disney's dog Pluto was sketched the same year the cosmic object was discovered. And Pluto was discovered by an American."

*

"Space in general gave us GPS - that's not specifically NASA, but it's investments in space."

*

"The universe is almost 14 billion years old, and, wow! Life had no problem starting here on Earth! I think it would be inexcusably egocentric of us to suggest that we're alone in the universe."

*

"When Kennedy said, 'Let's go to the moon,' we didn't yet have a vehicle that wouldn't kill you on launch. He said we'll land a man on the moon in eight years and bring him back. That was an audacious goal to put forth in front of the American people."

*

"The first colony on Mars is not going to be built by a private company. How are you going to make money? You're not."

*

"Philosophically, the universe has really never made things in ones. The Earth is special and everything else is different? No, we've got seven other planets. The sun? No, the sun is one of those dots in the night sky. The Milky Way? No, it's one of a hundred billion galaxies. And the universe - maybe it's one of countless other universes."

*

"As a scientist, I want to go to Mars and back to asteroids and the Moon because I'm a scientist. But I can tell you, I'm not so naive a scientist to think that the nation might not have geopolitical reasons for going into space."

*

"In any city with lots of skyscrapers, lots of skyline, the moon seems bigger than it is. It's called the moon illusion."

*

"Pluto's orbit is so elongated that it crosses the orbit of another planet. Now that's... you've got no business doing that if you want to call yourself a planet. Come on, now! There's something especially transgressive about that."

*

"All of the full moons for the entire year are special in that they have particular names."

*

"The universe is hilarious! Like, Venus is 900 degrees. I could tell you it melts lead. But that's not as fun as saying, 'You can cook a pizza on the windowsill in nine seconds.' And next time my fans eat pizza, they're thinking of Venus!"

*

"There are thousands of asteroids whose orbit in the Solar System crosses that of Earth. And we have a little acronym for them - NEOs: near Earth objects. And our biggest goal is to try to catalogue them, so we know in advance if one is going to put us at risk."

*

"The Pacific is the best toilet for satellites."

*

"'Cosmos' is an occasion to bring everything that I have, all of my capacity to communicate. We may go to the edge of the universe, but we're going to land right on you: in your heart, in your soul, in your mind. My goal is to have people know that they are participants in this great unfolding cosmic story."

*

"The first trillionaire in the world will be the person who mines asteroids."

*

"No astrophysicist would deny the possibility of life. I think we're not creative enough to imagine what life would be like on another planet. Show me a dead alien. Better yet, show me a live one!"

GENERAL THOUGHTS & OPINIONS

"One of my great laments is that education today seems to be less about passion and more about process, more about tactic or technique."

*

"'Boldly going where hundreds have gone before' does not make headlines."

*

"I think the greatest of people in society carved niches that represented the unique expression of their combinations of talents, and if everyone had the luxury of expressing the unique combinations of talents in this world, our society would be transformed overnight."

*

"Big ideas, big ambitious projects need to be embedded within culture at a level deeper than the political winds. It needs to be deeper than the economic fluctuations that could turn people against an expensive project because they're on an unemployment line and can't feed their families."

*

"Somehow it's O.K. for people to chuckle about not being good at math. Yet if I said, 'I never learned to read,' they'd say I was an illiterate dolt."

*

"We live in the kind of society where, in almost all cases, hard work is rewarded."

*

"Perhaps we've never been visited by aliens because

they have looked upon Earth and decided there's no sign of intelligent life."

*

"Private enterprise in the history of civilization has never led large, expensive, dangerous projects with unknown risks. That has never happened because when you combine all these factors, you cannot create a capital market valuation of that activity."

*

"Not enough books focus on how a culture responds to radically new ideas or discovery. Especially in the biography genre, they tend to focus on all the sordid details in the life of the person who made the discovery. I find this path to be voyeuristic but not enlightening."

*

"Even with all our technology and the inventions that make modern life so much easier than it once was, it takes just one big natural disaster to wipe all that away and remind us that, here on Earth, we're still at the mercy of nature."

FRANK JOHNSON

*

"No one wants to die, and no one wants to die poor. These are the two fundamental truths that transcend culture, they transcend politics, they transcend economic cycles."

*

"I said that if an alien came to visit, I'd be embarrassed to tell them that we fight wars to pull fossil fuels out of the ground to run our transportation. They'd be like, 'What?'"

*

"We have bred multiple generations of people who have not experienced knowing where you are the moment a news story broke, with that news story being great and grand and something that elevates society instead of diminishes it."

*

"The history of exploration has never been driven by exploration. But Columbus himself was a discoverer.

So was Magellan. But the people who wrote checks were not. They had other motivations."

*

"Many academicians don't even own a television, much less watch one."

*

"Stephen Hawking's been watching too many Hollywood movies. I think the only kind aliens in Hollywood are the ones created by Steven Spielberg - 'Close Encounters of the Third Kind' and 'E.T.,' for example. All other aliens are trying to suck our brains out."

*

"I don't know anybody who said, 'I love that teacher, he or she gave a really good homework set,' or 'Boy, that was the best class I ever took because those exams were awesome.' That's not what people want to talk about. It's not what influences people in one profession or another."

*

"People generally don't recognize how long it takes to conceive, publish, and write a book."

MANKIND

"The cross pollination of disciplines is fundamental to truly revolutionary advances in our culture."

*

"It's part of our pop culture to give animals human personalities and talents."

*

"We are part of this universe; we are in this universe, but perhaps more important than both of those facts, is that the universe is in us."

*

"Humans aren't as good as we should be in our capacity to empathize with feelings and thoughts of others, be they humans or other animals on Earth."

*

"I know of no time in human history where ignorance was better than knowledge."

*

"It turns out our brain is sensitive, maybe too sensitive, to motion. It's a survival mechanism."

*

"Everything we do, every thought we've ever had, is produced by the human brain. But exactly how it operates remains one of the biggest unsolved mysteries, and it seems the more we probe its secrets, the more surprises we find."

*

"In all civilizations we've studied, all cultures that we know of across the Earth and across time have invested some kind of attempt to understanding where where, where they come from, and where they are going."

*

"For centuries, magicians have intuitively taken advantage of the inner workings of our brains."

*

"Just think for how long humanity was controlled by mystical, magical thinking - the diseases and suffering that led to. We managed to survive, but just barely. It wasn't pretty."

*

"The most creative people are motivated by the grandest of problems that are presented before them."

*

"It may be that our cosmic curiosity... is a genetically-encoded force that we illuminate when we look up and wonder."

*

"Humans aren't as good as we should be in our capacity to empathize with feelings and thoughts of others, be they humans or other animals on Earth. So maybe part of our formal education should be training in empathy. Imagine how different the world would be if, in fact, that were 'reading, writing, arithmetic, empathy.'"

*

"The history of exploration across nations and across time is not one where nations said, 'Let's explore because it's fun.' It was, 'Let's explore so that we can claim lands for our country, so that we can open up new trade routes; let's explore so we can become more powerful.'"

*

"It's always interesting just to see how the human mind is relating to the natural universe, and what we try to make of it just so we can believe we understand what's going on."

PHILOSOPHY

"We define ourselves as intelligent. That's odd, because we're doing the definition - We're creating our own definition and saying, 'We are intelligent!'"

*

"In the animal kingdom, one of the keys to survival is to outwit your enemies. And when you're surrounded by carnivores, one of the best strategies is to fade into the background and disappear."

*

"We live on this speck called Earth - think about what you might do, today or tomorrow - and make the most of it."

*

"No one is dumb who is curious. The people who don't ask questions remain clueless throughout their lives."

*

"Not enough people in this world, I think, carry a cosmic perspective with them. It could be life-changing."

*

"Rational thoughts never drive people's creativity the way emotions do."

*

"If you think of feelings you have when you are awed by something - for example, knowing that elements in your body trace to exploded stars - I call that a spiritual reaction, speaking of awe and majesty, where words fail you."

*

"I think the greatest of people that have ever been in society, they were never versions of someone else. They were themselves."

*

"Passion is what gets you through the hardest times that might otherwise make strong men weak, or make you give up."

*

"It's the great tragedy - people employed in ways that don't fully tap everything they do best in life."

*

"What you need, above all else, is a love for your subject, whatever it is. You've got to be so deeply in love with your subject that when curve balls are thrown, when hurdles are put in place, you've got the energy to overcome them."

*

"We didn't build the interstate system to connect New York to Los Angeles because the West Coast was a priority. No, we webbed the highways so people can go to multiple places and invent ways of doing things not thought of by the persons building the roads."

*

"Being at the top of your game intellectually, philosophically, politically, is not a forever thing."

*

"I think that intelligence is such a narrow branch of the tree of life - this branch of primates we call humans. No other animal, by our definition, can be considered intelligent. So intelligence can't be all that important for survival, because there are so many animals that don't have what we call intelligence, and they're surviving just fine."

*

"Typically, when you look for role models, you want

someone who has your interests and came from the same background. Well, look how restricting that is. What people should do is take role models a la carte. If there's someone whose character you appreciated, you respect that trait."

*

"There is no greater education than one that is self-driven."

*

"If your ego starts out, 'I am important, I am big, I am special,' you're in for some disappointments when you look around at what we've discovered about the universe. No, you're not big. No, you're not. You're small in time and in space. And you have this frail vessel called the human body that's limited on Earth."

*

"Everyone should have their mind blown once a day."

POLITICS

"You can't have people making decisions about the future of the world who are scientifically illiterate. That's a recipe for disaster. And I don't mean just whether a politician is scientifically literate, but people who vote politicians into office."

*

"When everyone agrees to a single solution and a single plan, there's nothing more efficient in the world than an efficient democracy."

*

"The only driver stronger than an economic argument

to do something is the war argument, the I-don't-want-to-die argument."

*

"You have not fully expressed your power as a voter until you have scientific literacy in topics that matter for future political issues."

*

"When you put money directly to a problem, it makes a good headline. It makes a good campaign slogan. You get to claim that you've engaged in these activities within an election cycle. But certain investments take longer than an election cycle."

*

"The problem is that many people operate on the assumption that NASA should go to Congress every year with hat in hand and justify it every year. Well, I see it as the greatest economic driver that there ever was. Economic drivers don't need justification."

*

"When an industry matures, it means it's not advancing, and of course the jobs go overseas. That's the obligation of the multi-national corporation: to put the factory where it can make the widget as cheap as possible. Don't get angry when a corporation does that; we've all bought into this concept. We live in a capitalistic society."

*

"Fortunately, there's another handy driver that has manifested itself throughout the history of cultures. The urge to want to gain wealth. That is almost as potent a driver as the urge to maintain your security. And that is how I view NASA going forward - as an investment in our economy."

*

"We didn't go to the moon to explore or because it was in our DNA or because we're Americans. We went because we were at war and we felt a threat."

FRANK JOHNSON

RELIGION

"There is no example of someone reading their scripture and saying, 'I have a prediction about the world that no one knows yet, because this gave me insight. Let's go test that prediction,' and have the prediction be correct."

*

"I can't gather around and talk about how much everybody in the room doesn't believe in God. I just don't - I don't have the energy for that, and so I... Agnostic separates me from the conduct of atheists whether or not there is strong overlap between the two categories, and at the end of the day I'd rather not be any category at all."

FRANK JOHNSON

*

"What people are really after is, what is my stance on religion or spirituality or God? And I would say, if I find a word that came closest, it would be agnostic."

*

"I'm perennially intrigued how people who lead largely evidence-based lives can, in a belief-based part of their mind, be certain that an invisible, divine entity created an entire universe just for us, or that the government is stockpiling space aliens in a secret desert location."

*

"If God is the mystery of the universe, these mysteries, we're tackling these mysteries one by one. If you're going to stay religious at the end of the conversation, God has to mean more to you than just where science has yet to tread."

*

"I'm constantly claimed by atheists. I find this intriguing. In fact, on my Wiki page - I didn't create the Wiki page, others did, and I'm flattered that people cared enough about my life to assemble it - and it said, 'Neil deGrasse is an atheist.'"

*

"It's actually the minority of religious people who rejects science or feel threatened by it or want to sort of undo or restrict the... where science can go. The rest, you know, are just fine with science. And it has been that way ever since the beginning."

*

"Most religious people in America fully embrace science. So the argument that religion has some issue with science applies to a small fraction of those who declare that they are religious. They just happen to be a very vocal fraction, so you got the impression that there are more of them than there actually is."

*

"So the history of discovery, particularly cosmic discovery, but discovery in general, scientific discovery, is one where at any given moment, there's a frontier. And there tends to be an urge for people, especially religious people, to assert that across that boundary, into the unknown, lies the handiwork of God. This shows up a lot."

*

"Most of what Einstein said and did has no direct impact on what anybody reads in the Bible. Special relativity, his work in quantum mechanics, nobody even knows or cares. Where Einstein really affects the Bible is the fact that general relativity is the organizing principle for the Big Bang."

*

"Every account of a higher power that I've seen described, of all religions that I've seen, include many statements with regard to the benevolence of that power. When I look at the universe and all the ways the universe wants to kill us, I find it hard to reconcile that with statements of beneficence."

FRANK JOHNSON

IN THE WORDS OF NEIL DEGRASSE TYSON

ALSO BY FRANK JOHNSON

INSIDE THE MIND OF EMMA WATSON

THE VERY BEST OF MAYA ANGELOU

THE WIT AND WISDOM OF DOLLY PARTON

THE VERY BEST OF VIVIENNE WESTWOOD